Faces of Pushkar

A Photo journey to the land of sand, camels, turbans and moustaches.

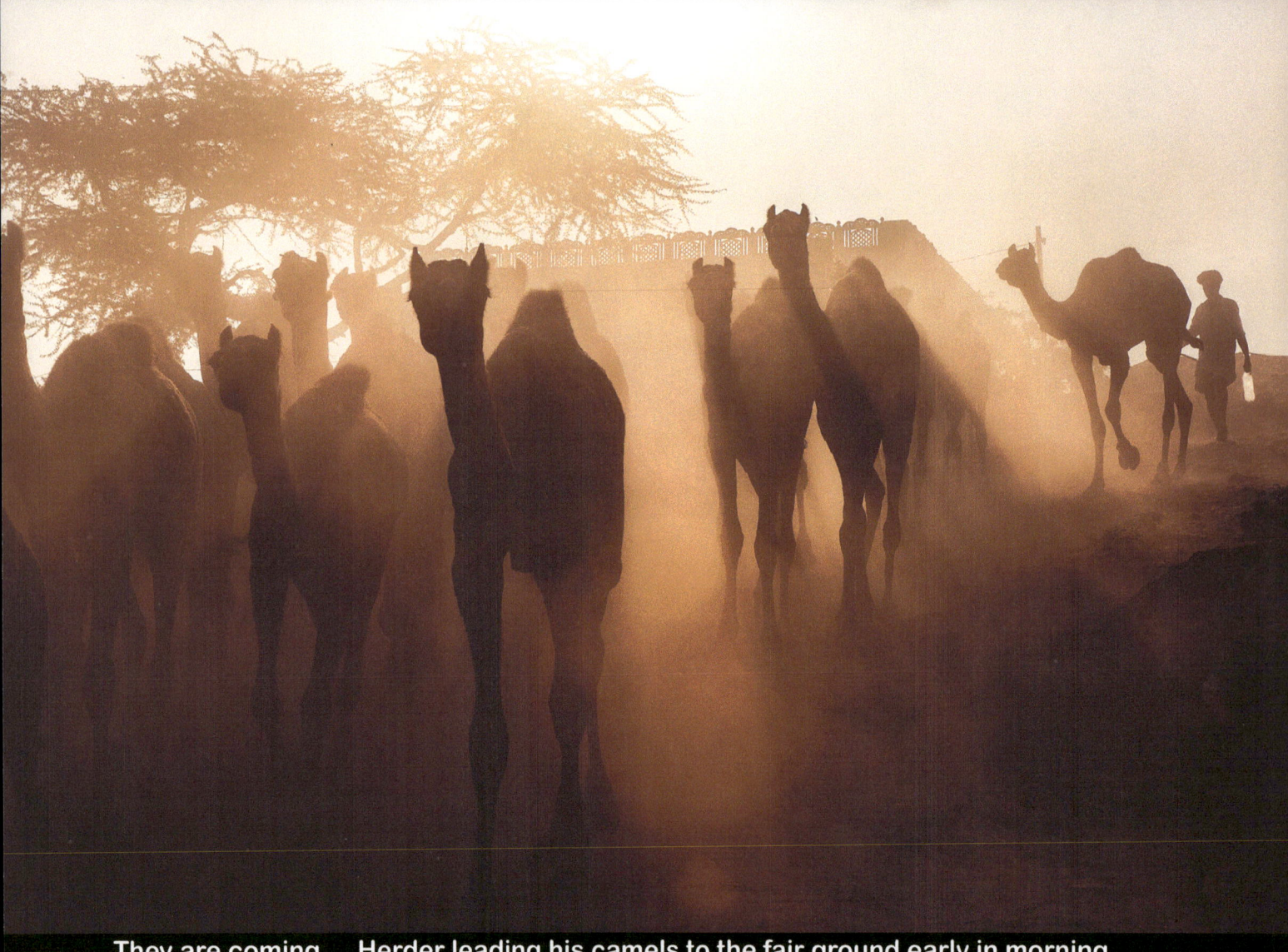

They are coming ... Herder leading his camels to the fair ground early in morning

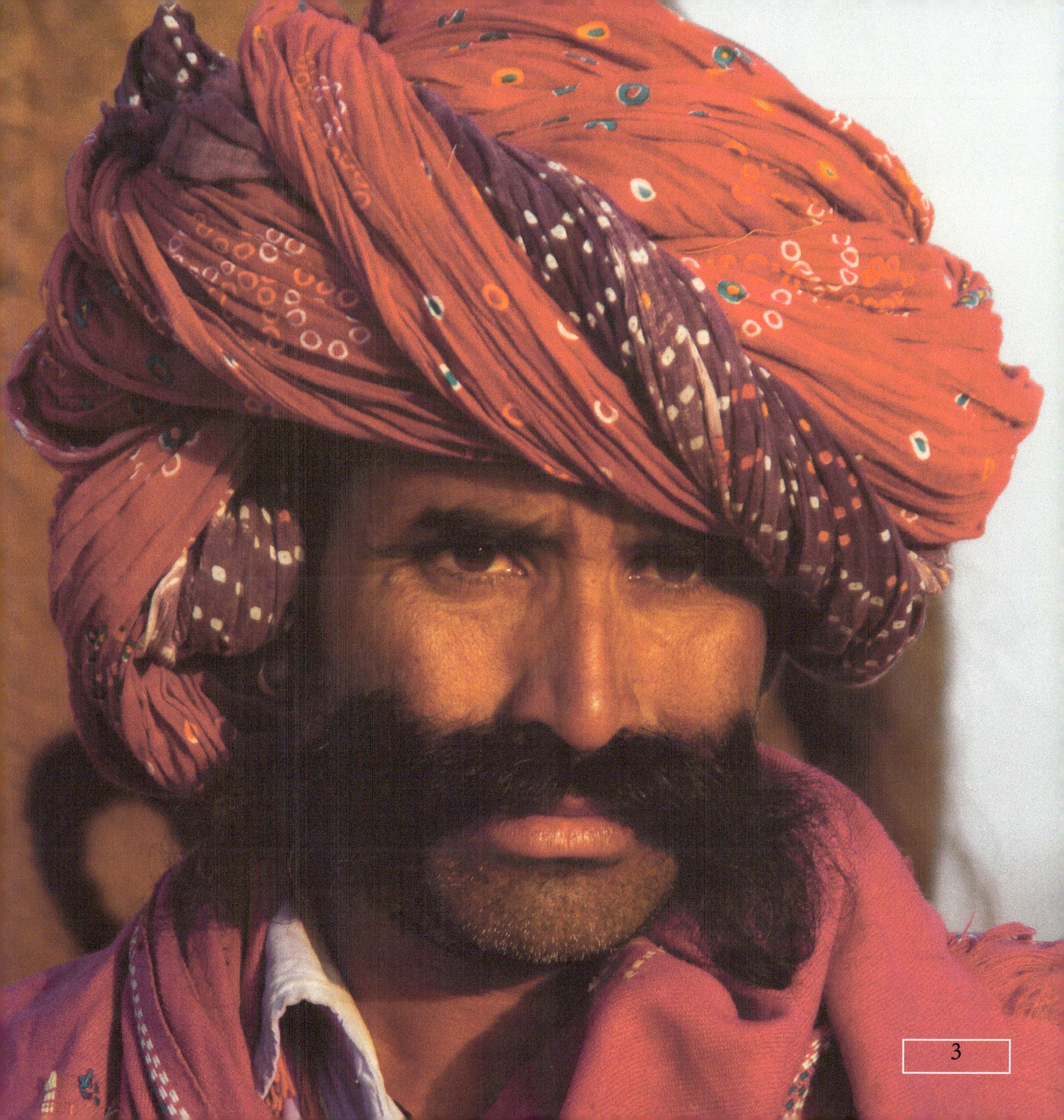

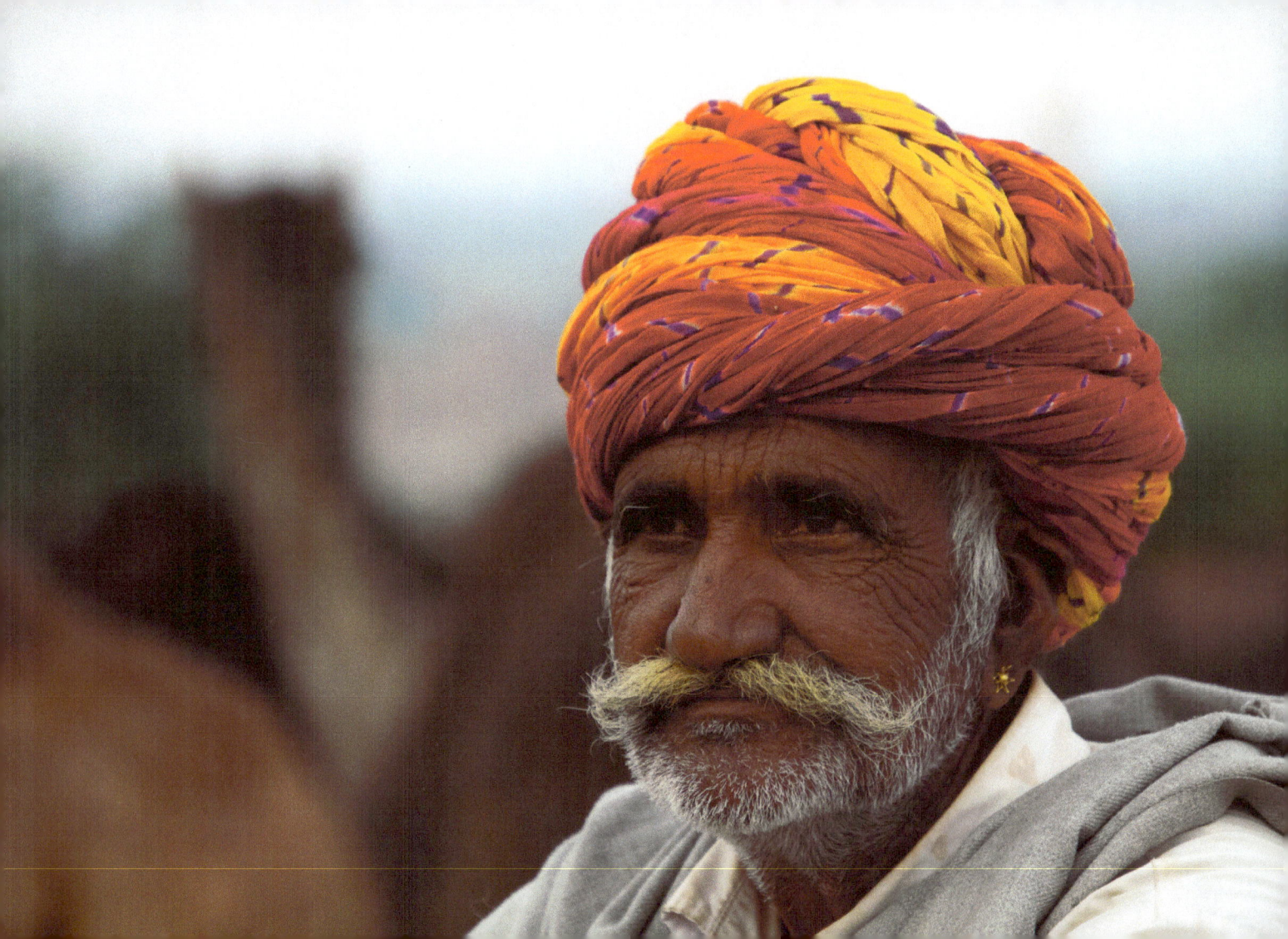

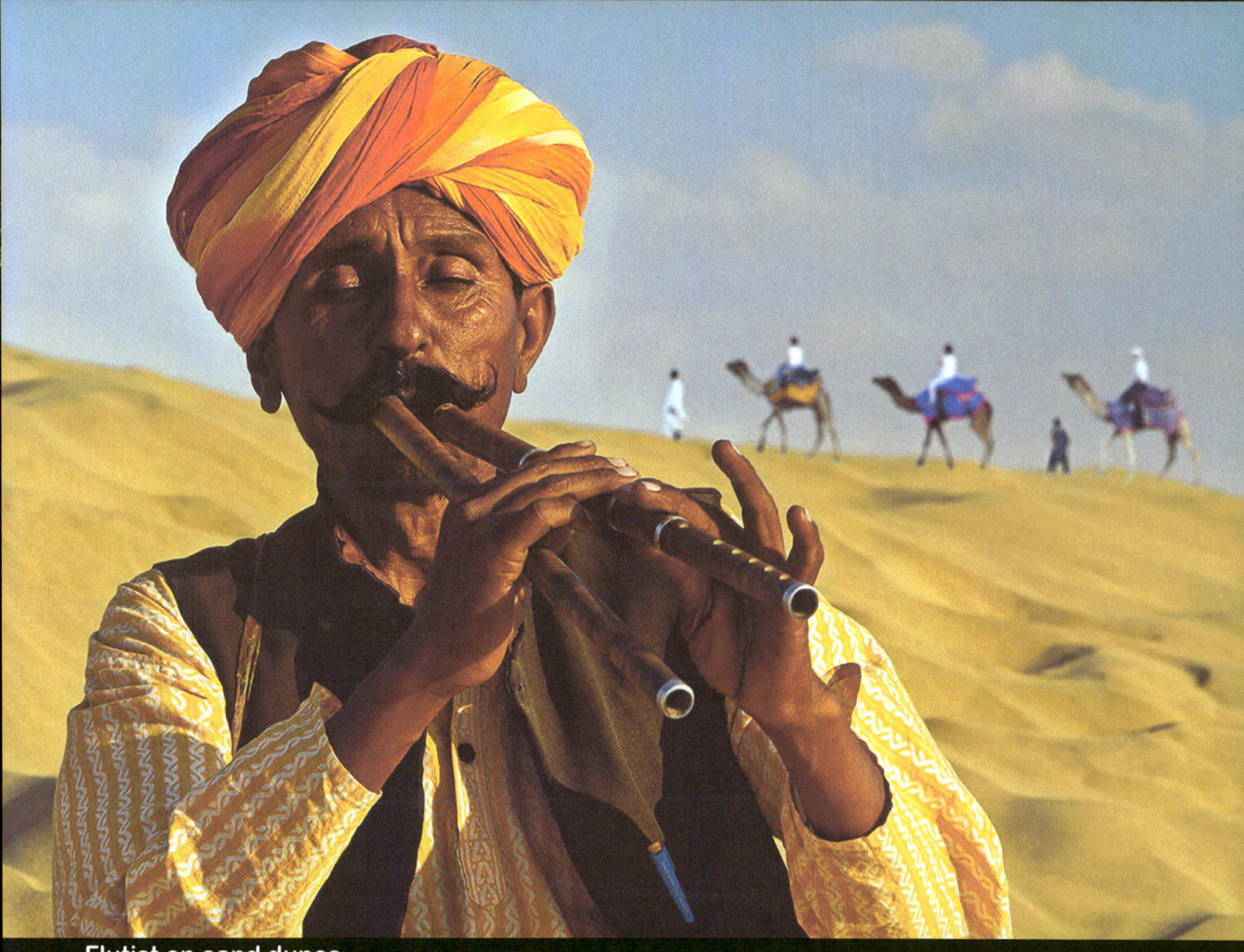
Flutist on sand dunes…

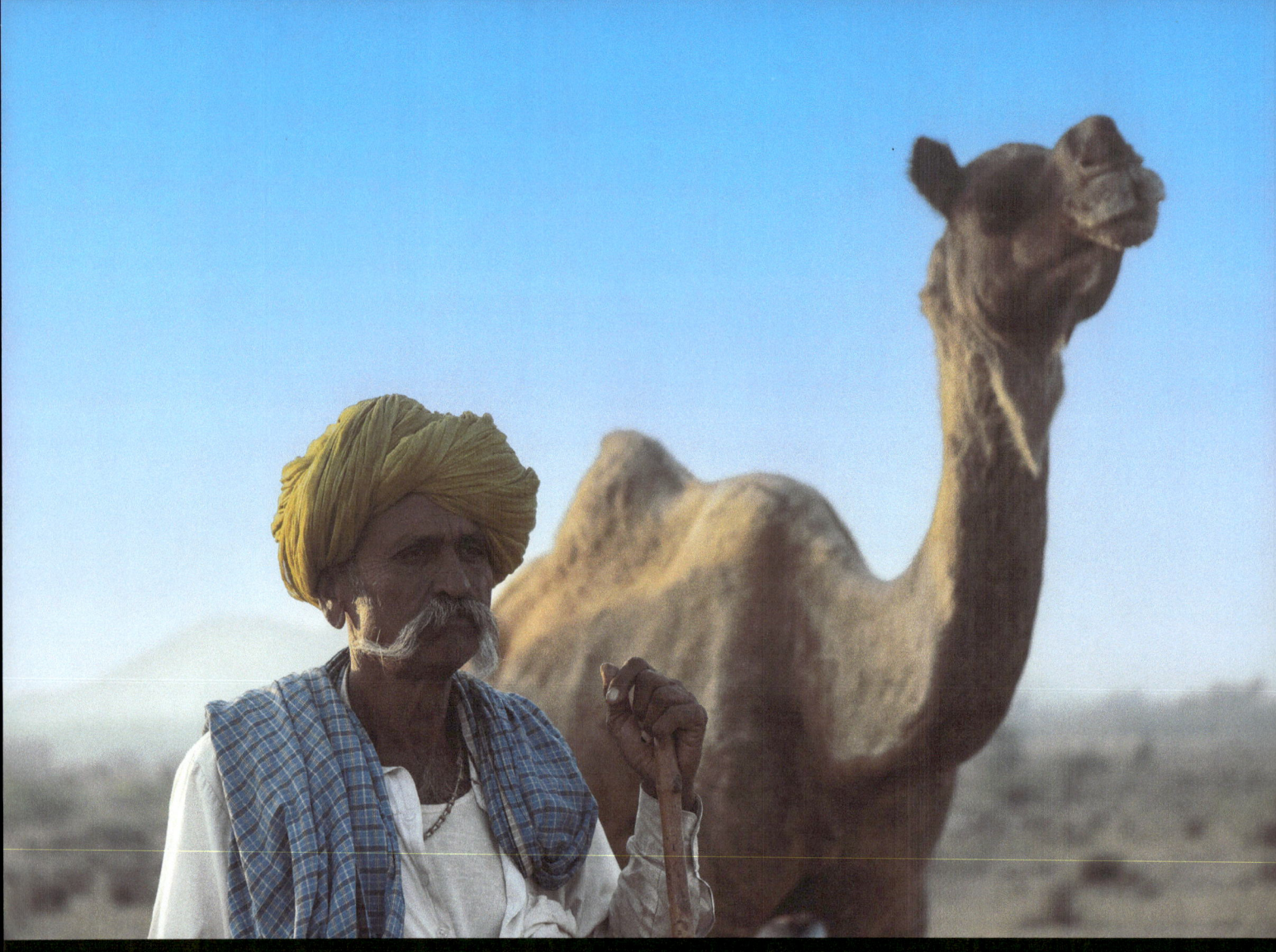
'Muchhad' Tauji with his camel..

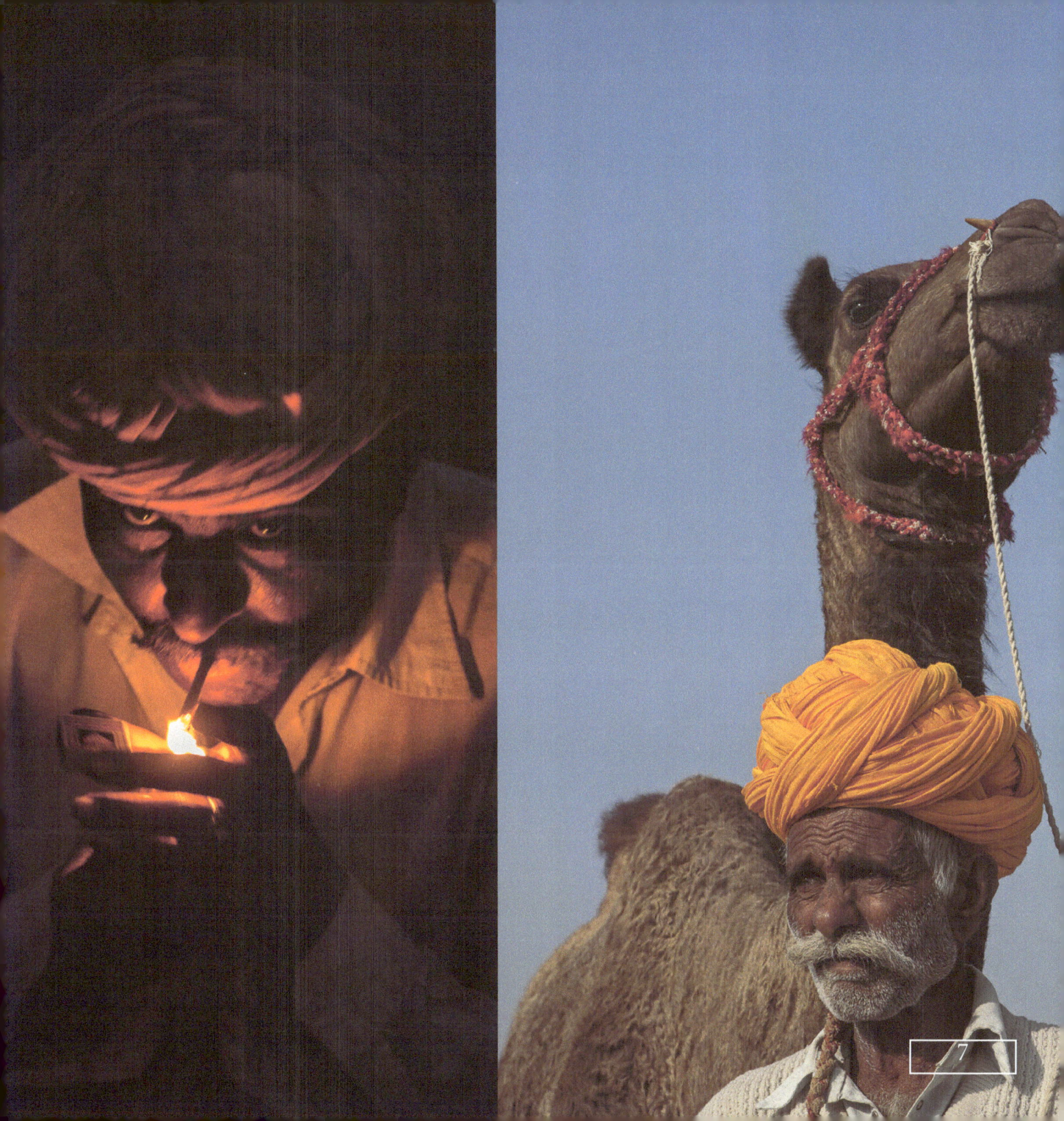

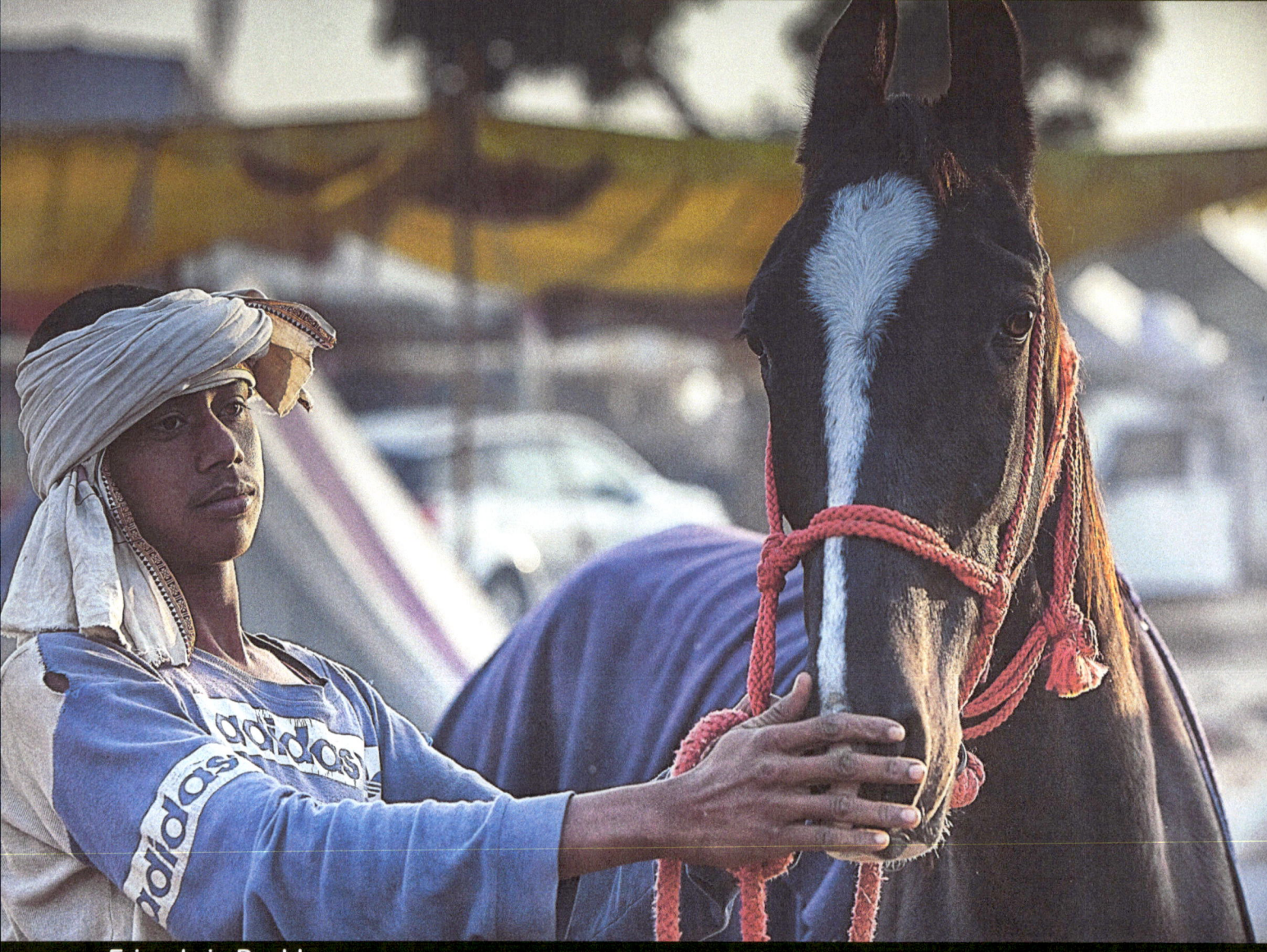
Friends in Pushkar

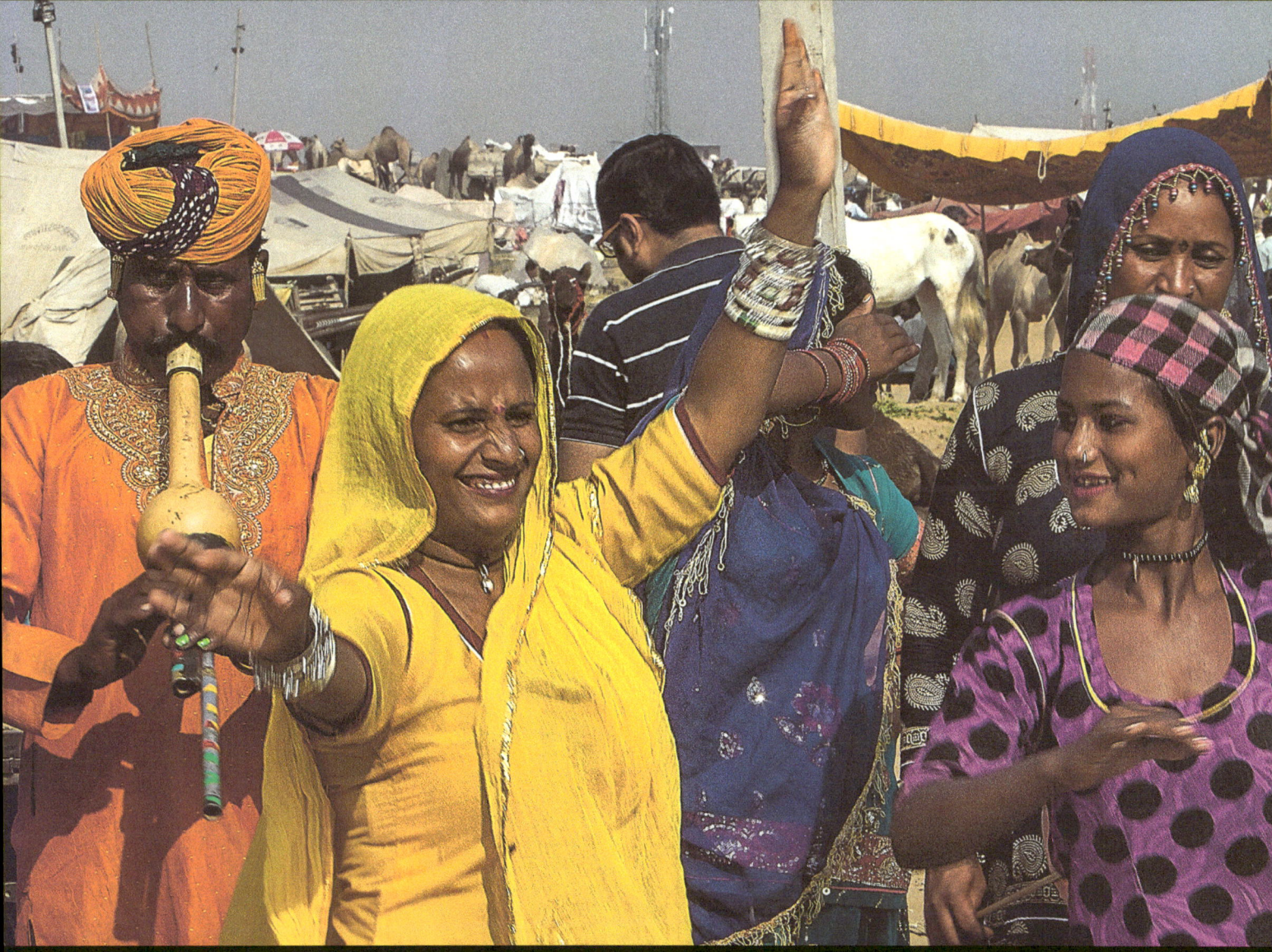
Happy faces in Pushkar.

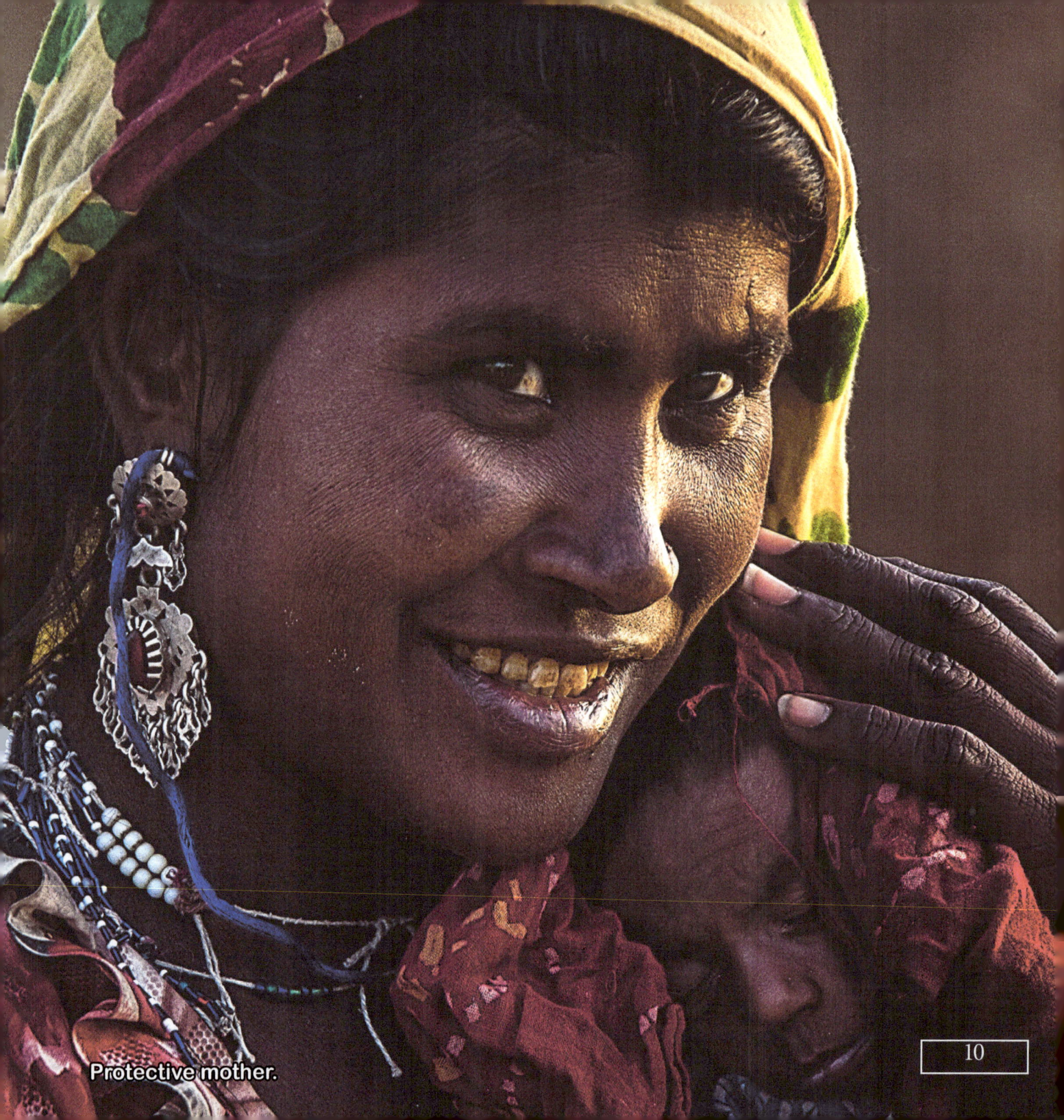
Protective mother.

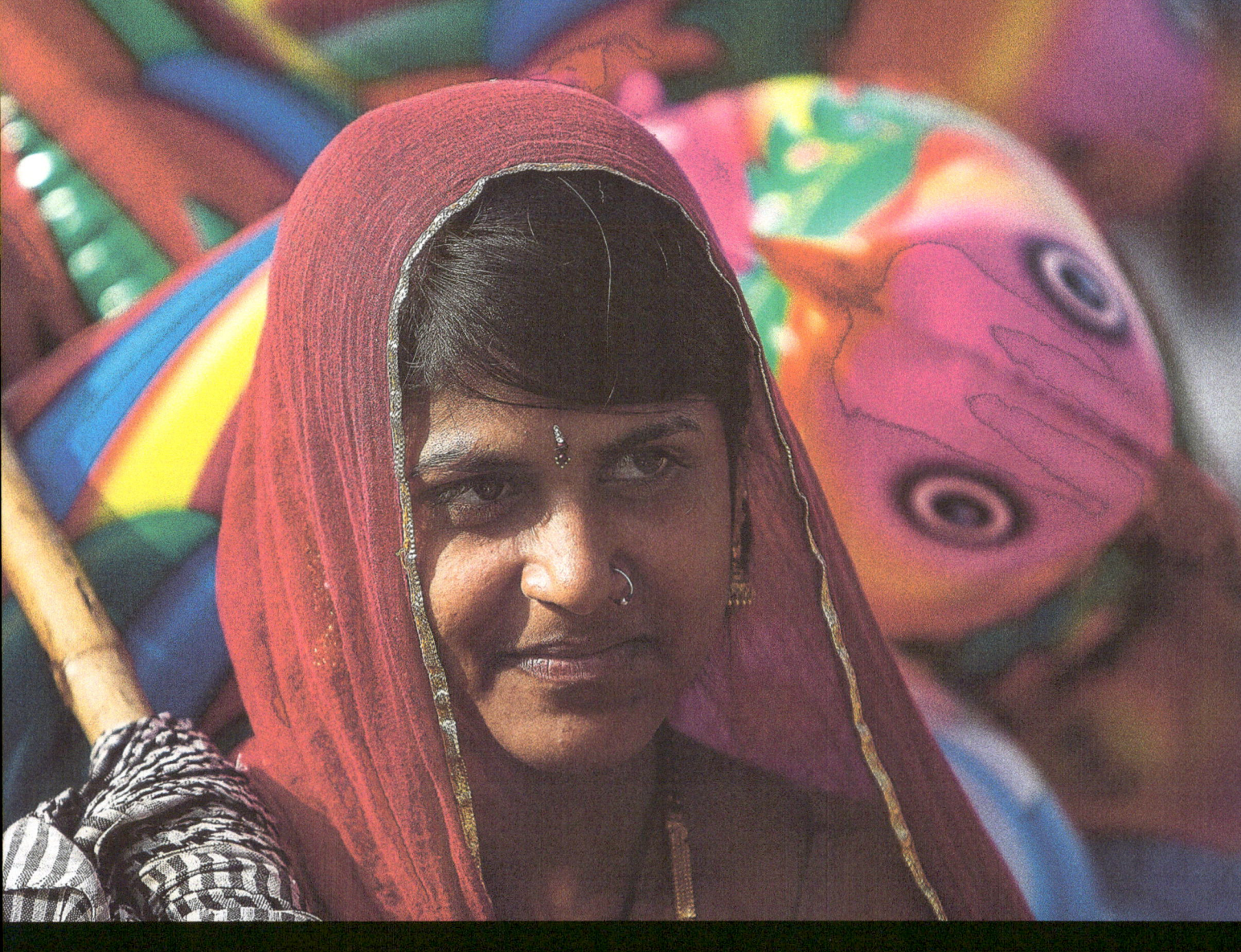

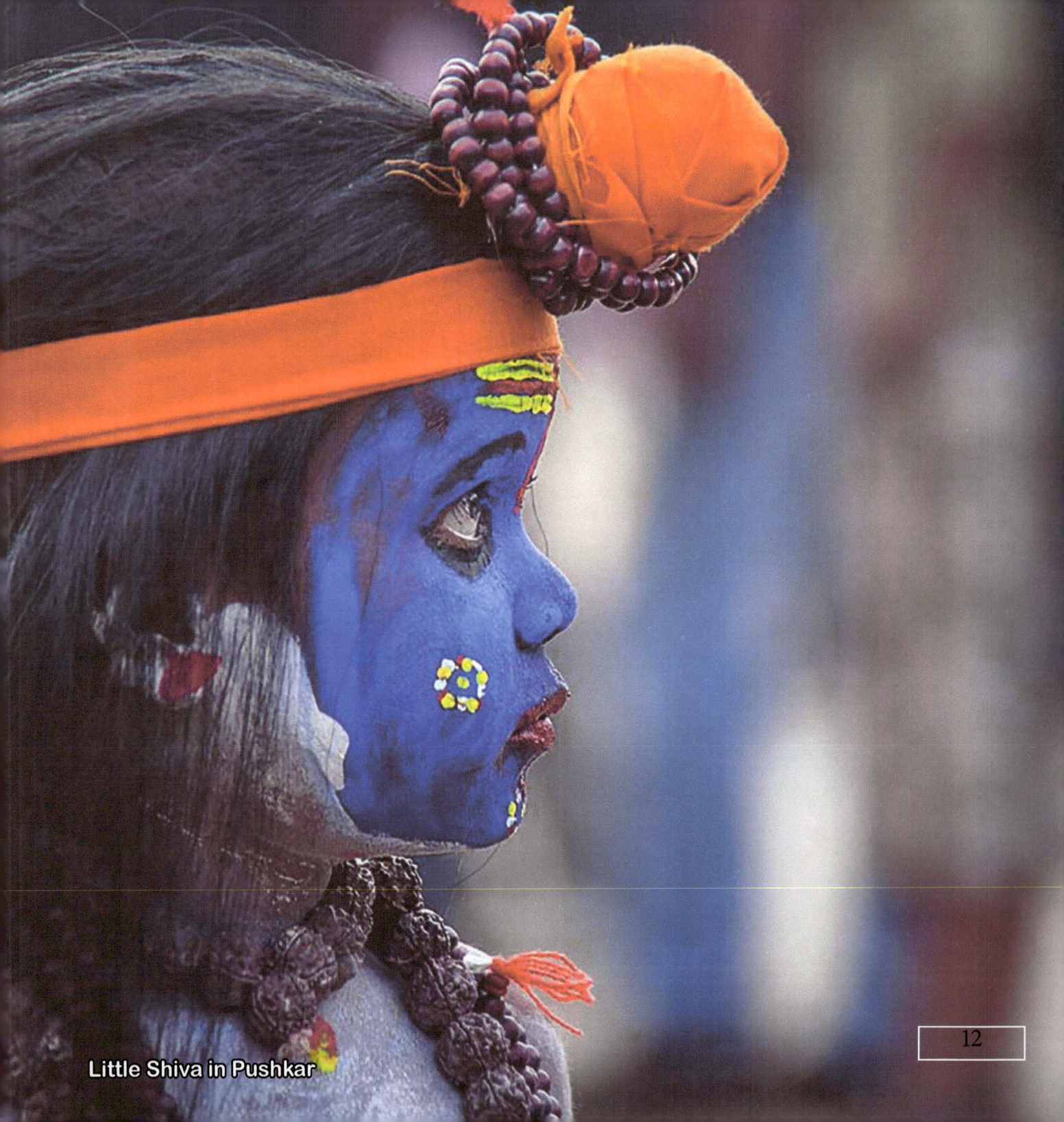
Little Shiva in Pushkar

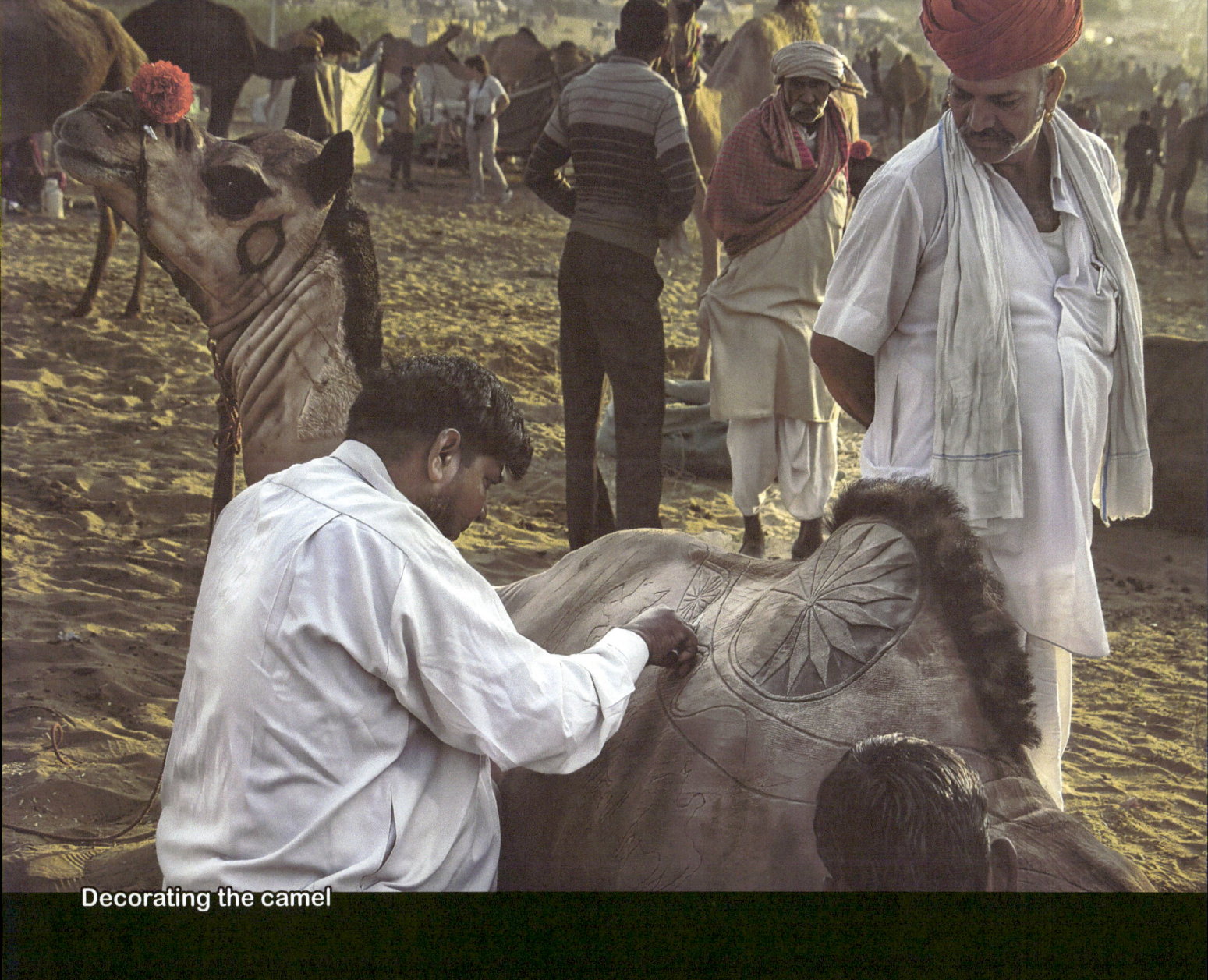
Decorating the camel

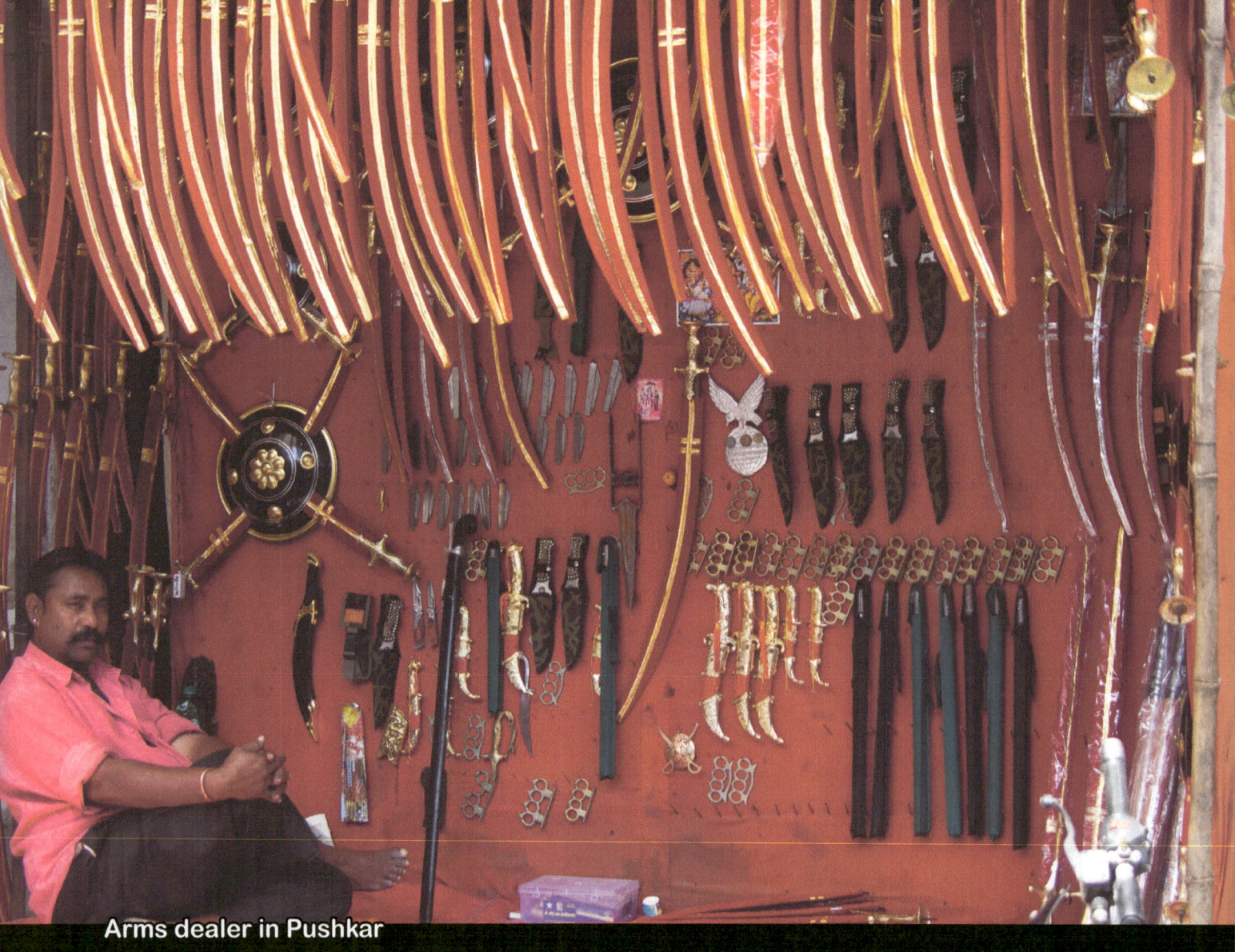
Arms dealer in Pushkar

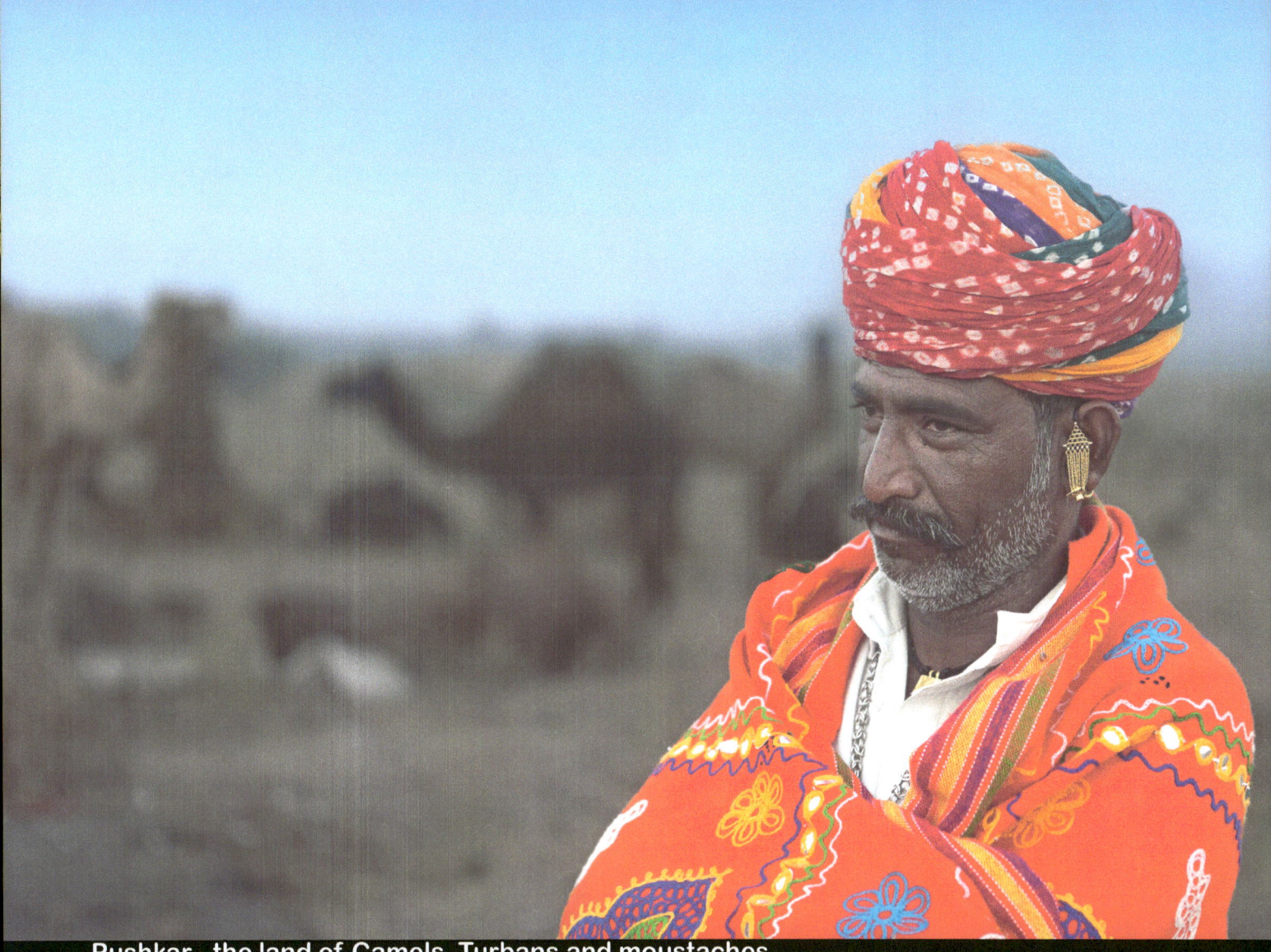
Pushkar...the land of Camels, Turbans and moustaches

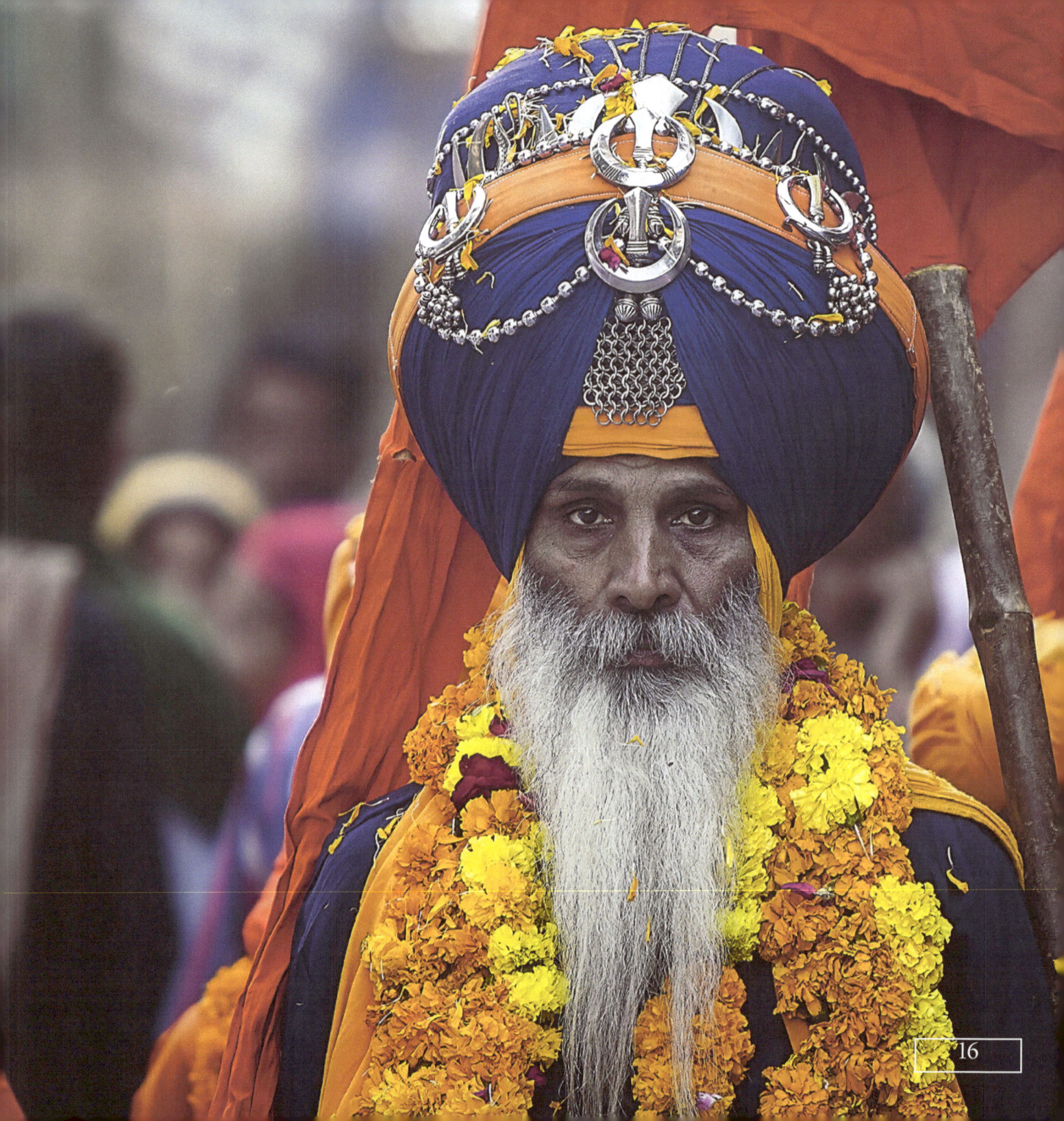

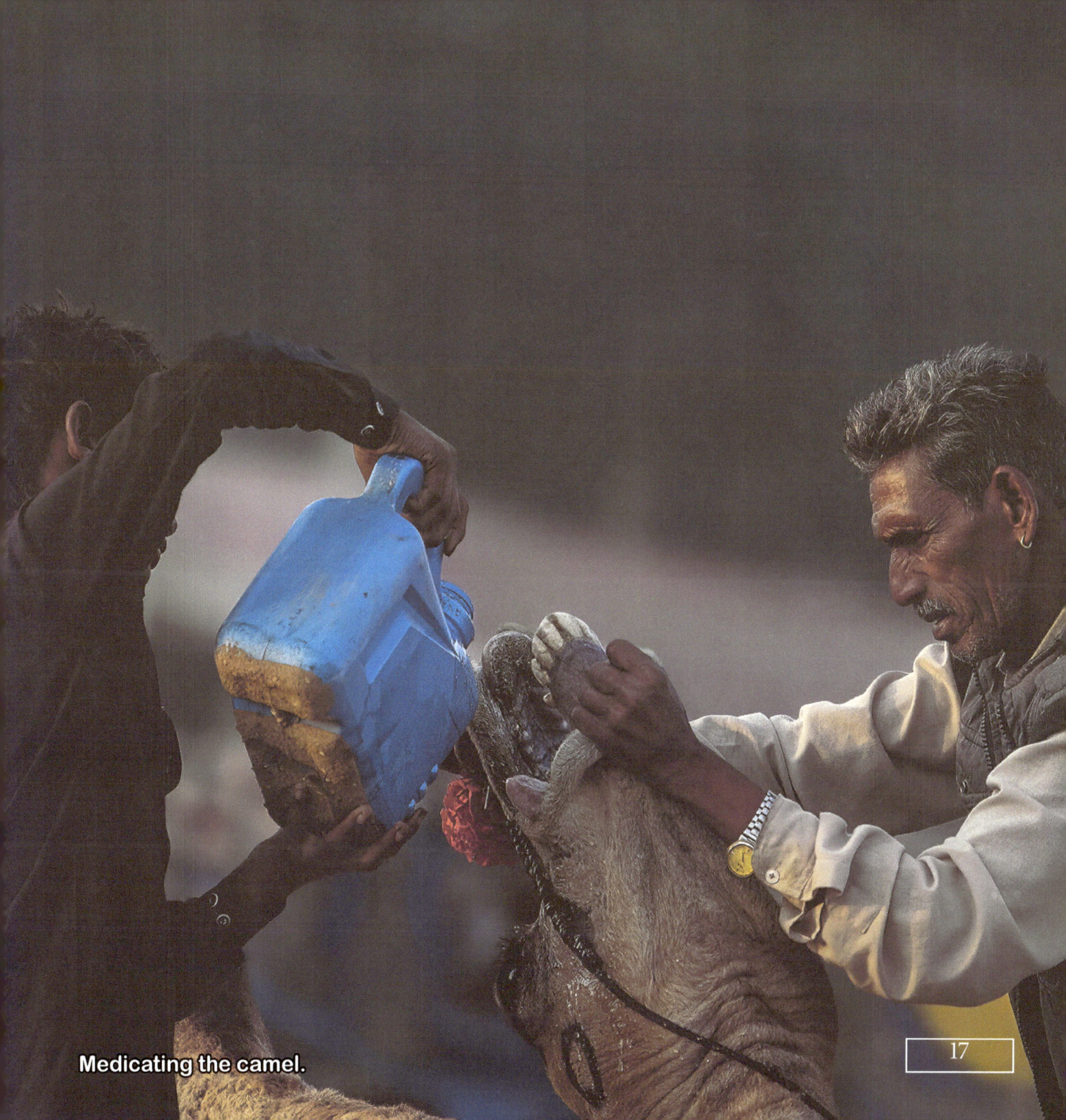
Medicating the camel.

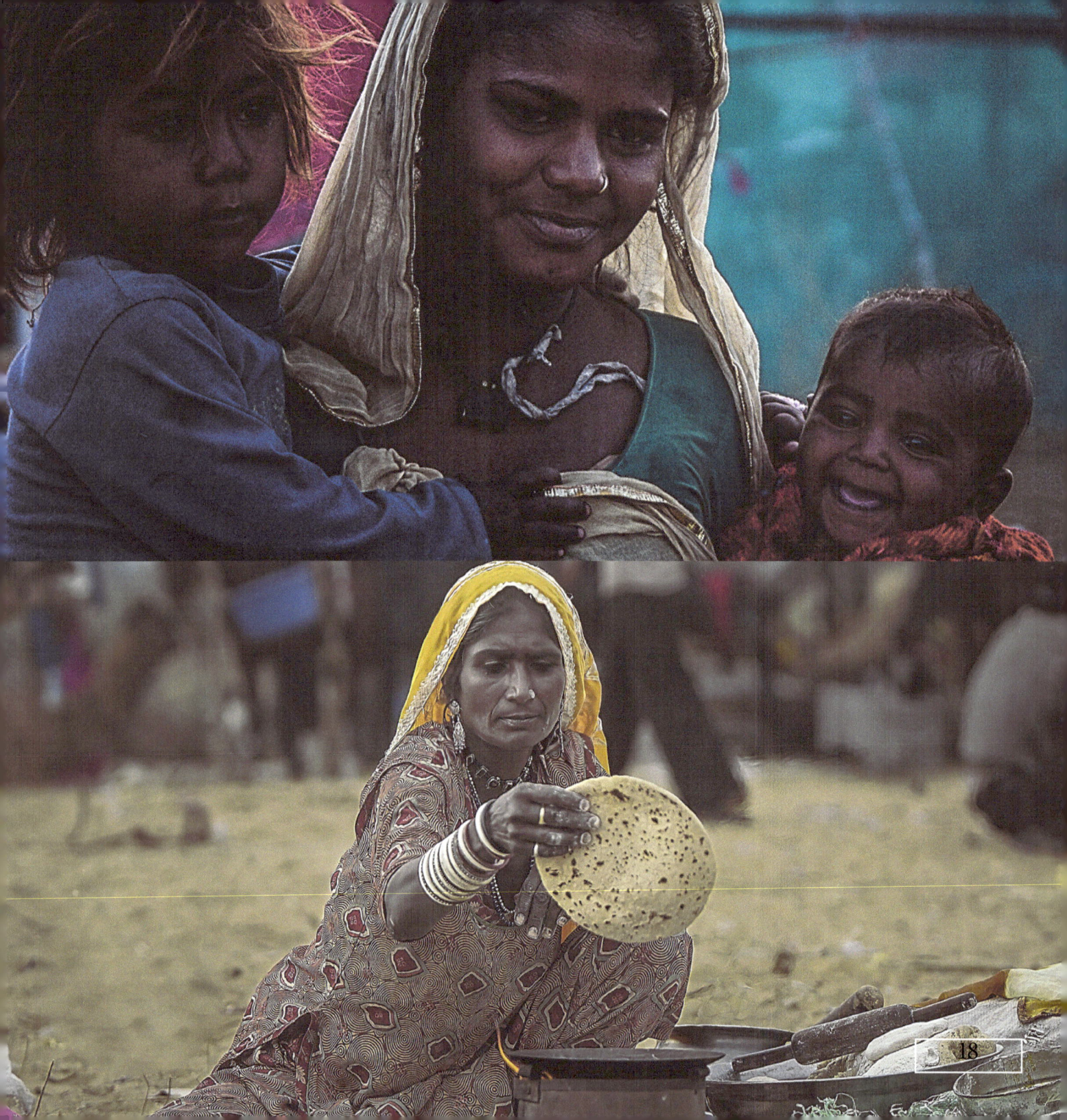

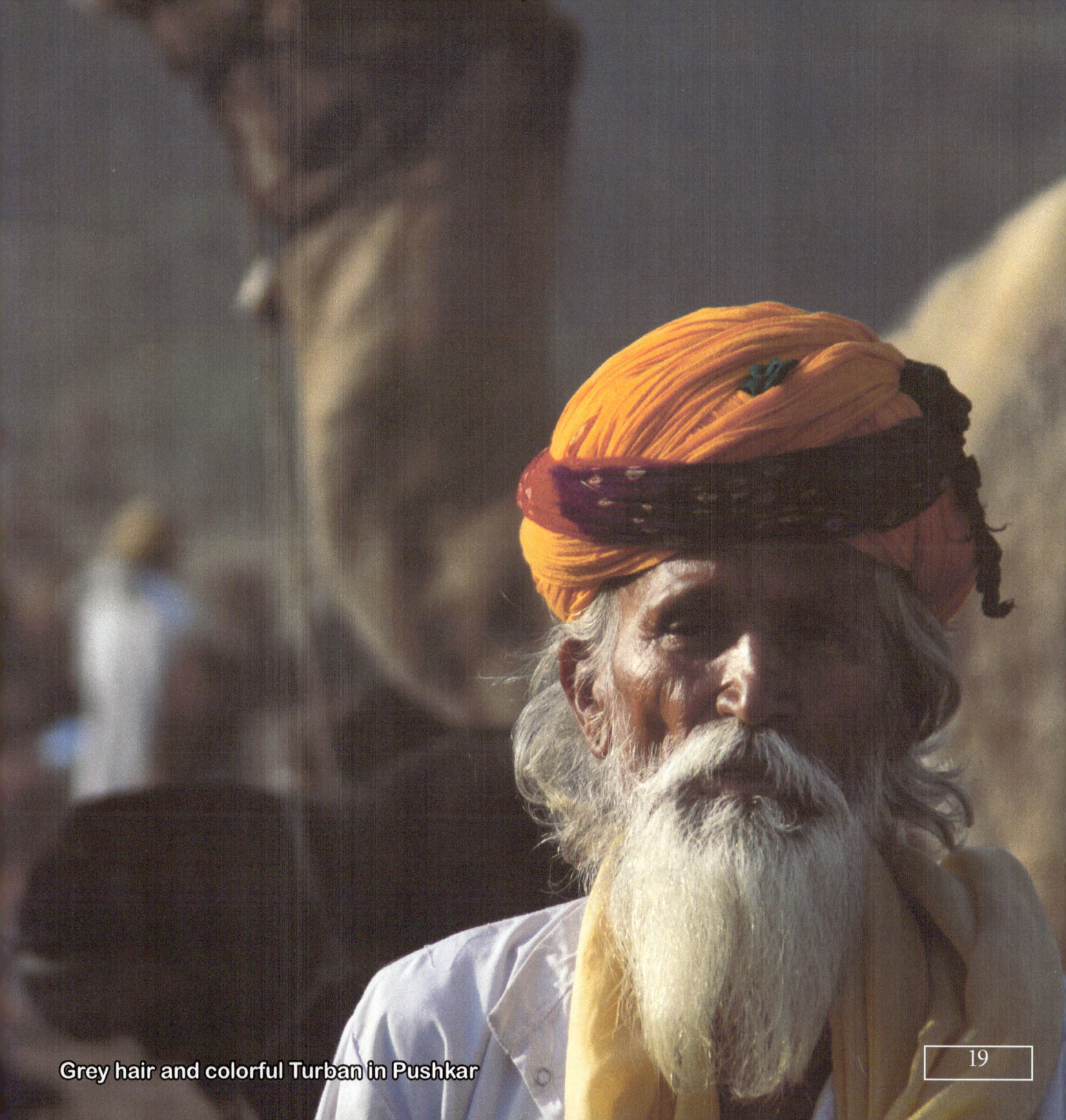
Grey hair and colorful Turban in Pushkar

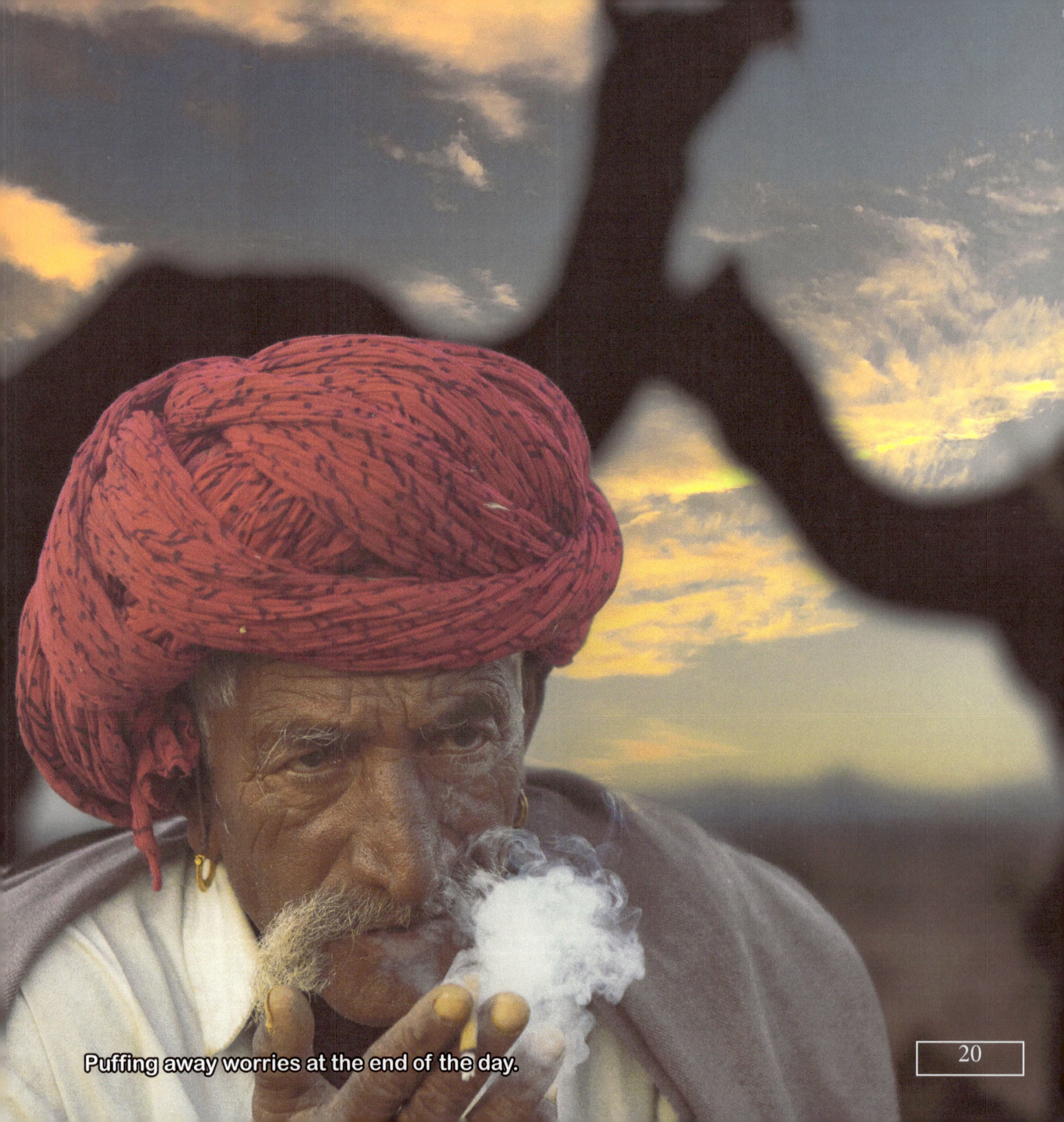
Puffing away worries at the end of the day.

20

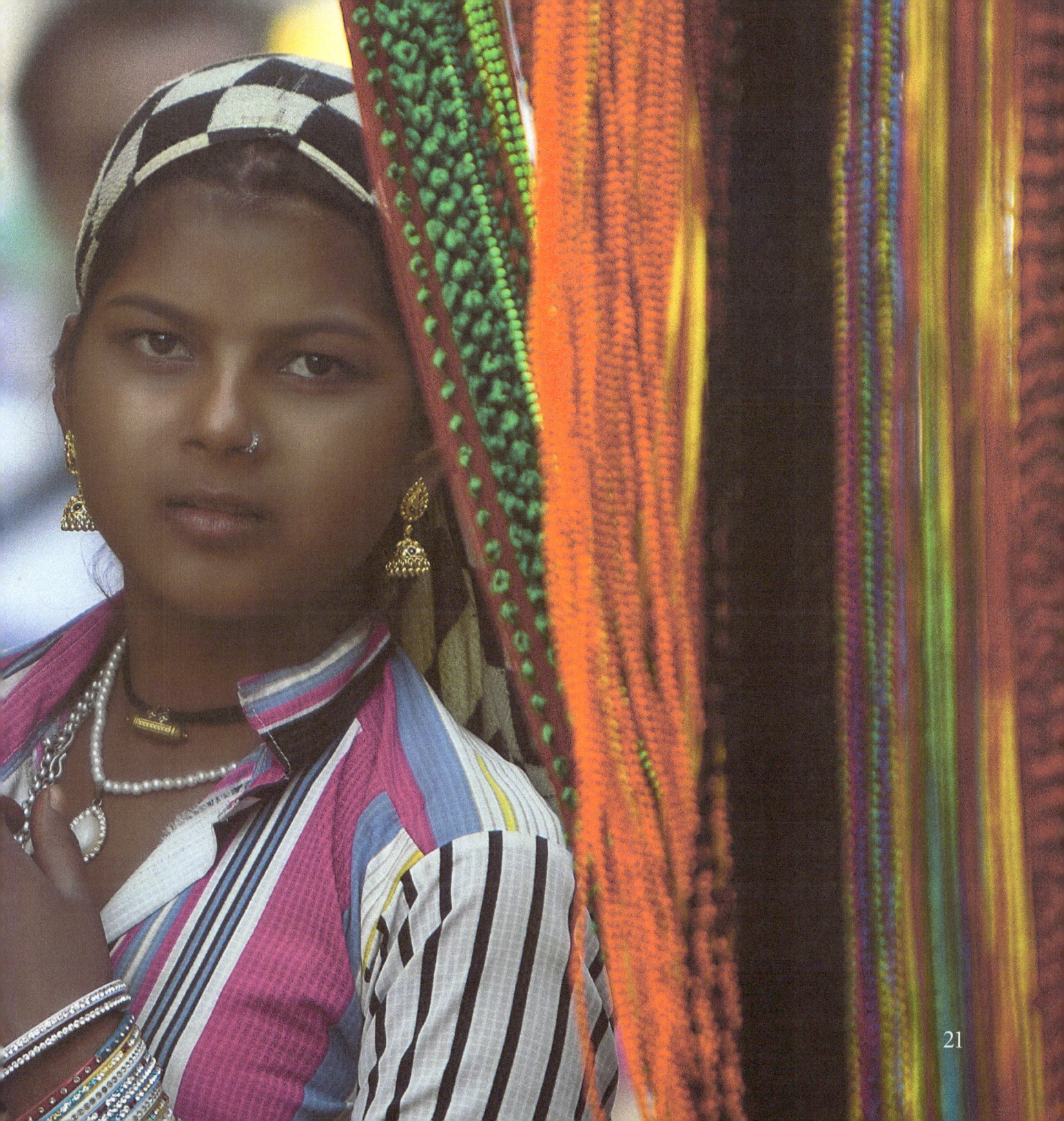

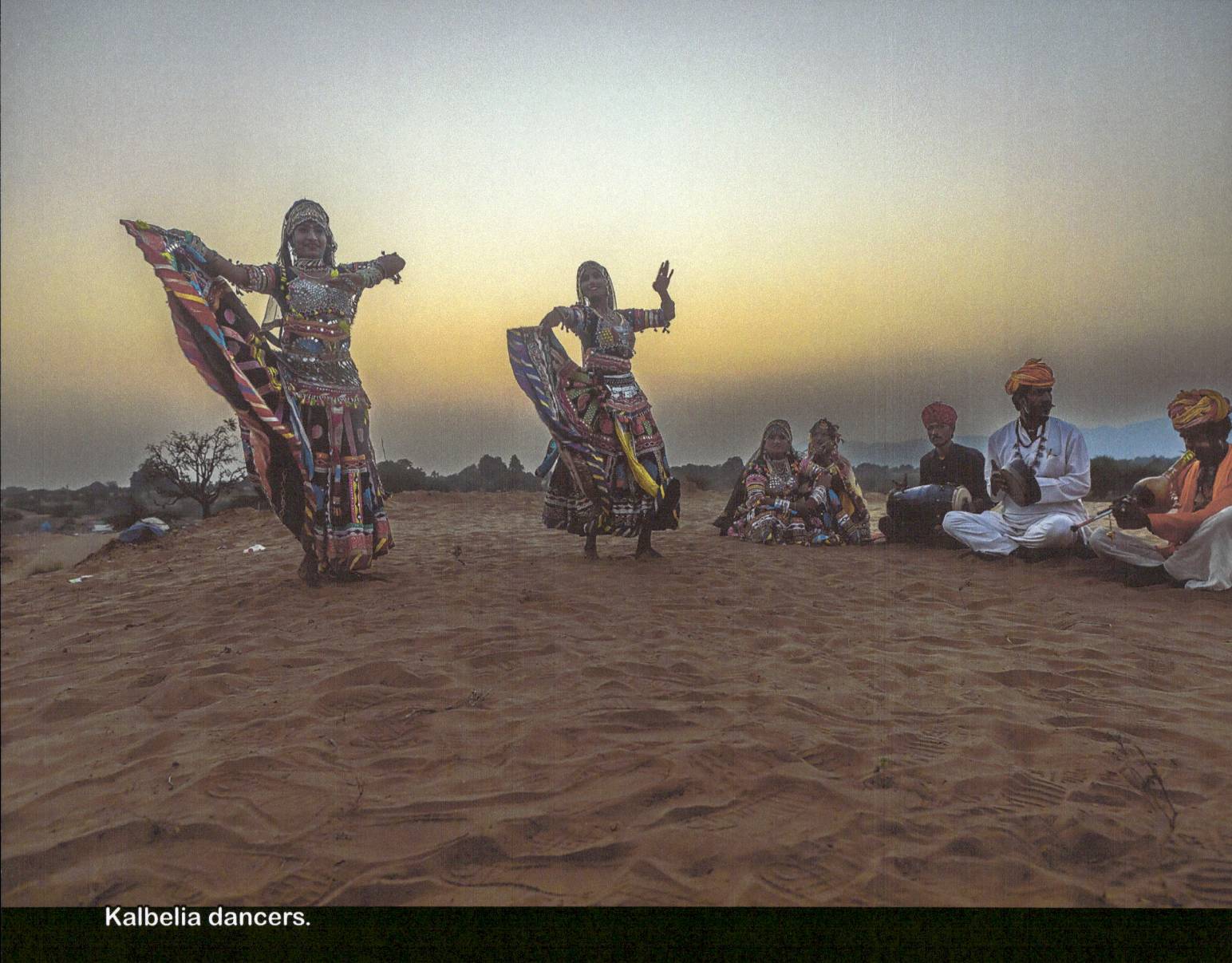
Kalbelia dancers.

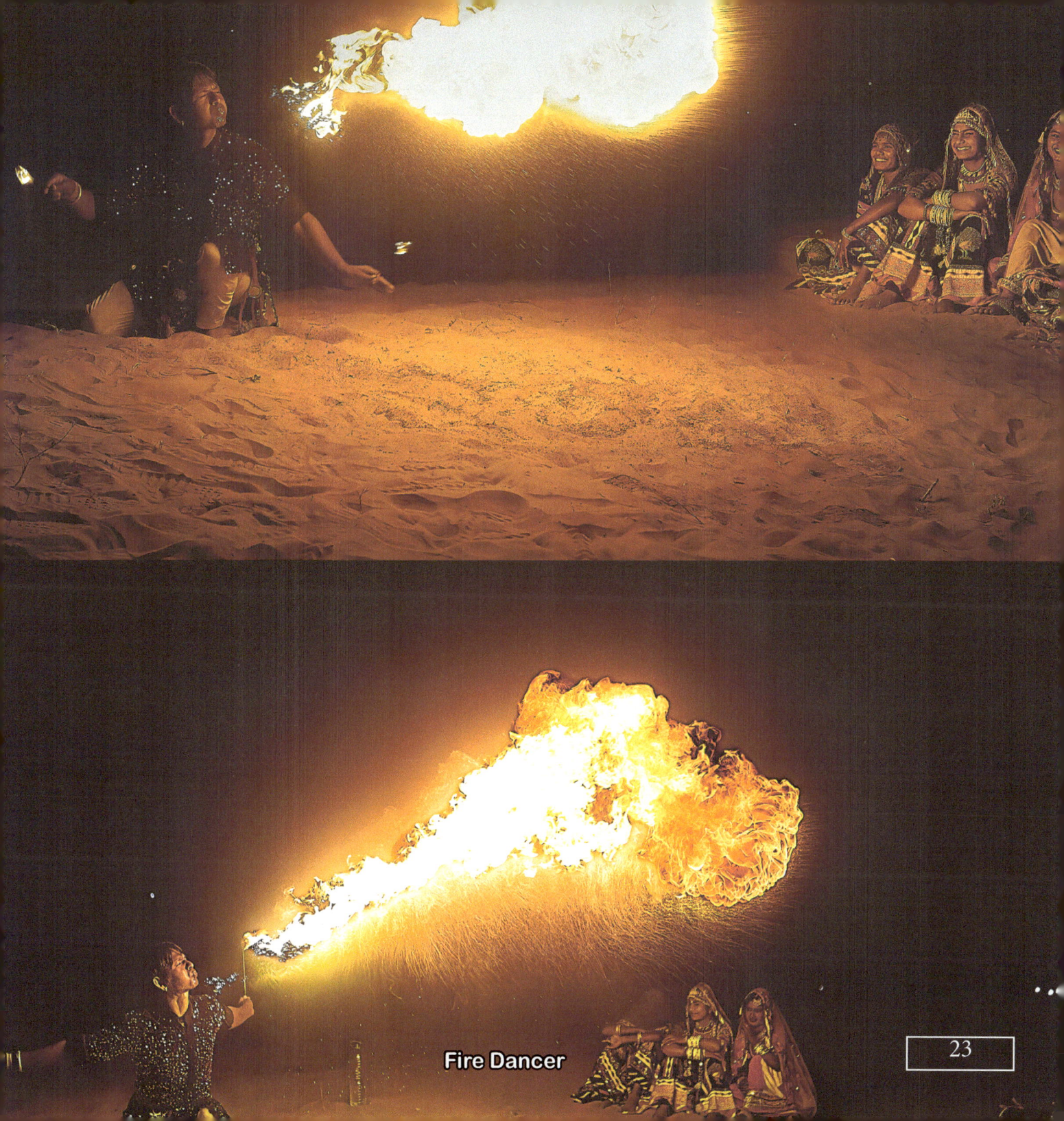
Fire Dancer

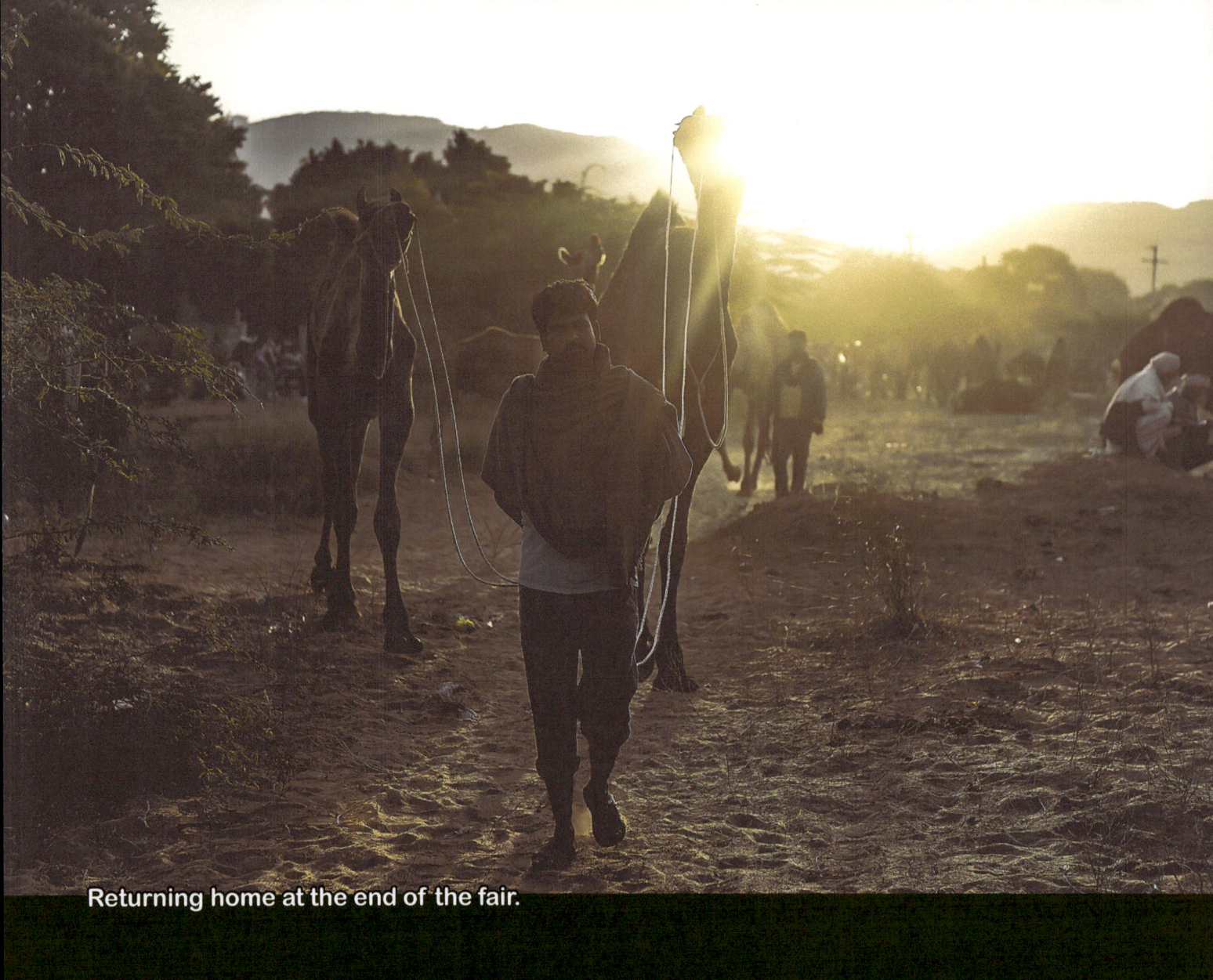
Returning home at the end of the fair.